# Ice Cream Recipes To Die For

## To Die For

Best Banana Ice Cream Cookbook You

Will Ever Find

# Table of Contents

# Introduction

Making sweet desserts can be very simple and easy now. Once you start making banana ice creams, you can't stop making and eating them. They are creamy, delicious, and most importantly, very healthy. They can be made entirely vegan and with wholesome sweeteners such as maple syrup, date syrup, honey, or agave syrup.

You can use different flavors such as nut butter, fruits, or chopped nuts of your choice to make everything more fun and entertaining for you and your family. Don't wait anymore! Grab your blender, place some simple everyday ingredients, and cook up a storm for your loved ones.

# 1. Classic Banana Ice Cream

When it comes to frozen desserts, this is probably one of the easiest and most simple ice cream recipes you will ever find. This recipe is used as a base for other flavored ice creams. Just two ingredients make a perfect summer dessert you can't say no to.

**Time:** 10 minutes

**Servings:** 4

**The list of ingredients:**

- 5 bananas (sliced and frozen)

- 4 tablespoons almond milk

- 1/2 teaspoon vanilla extract

**Methods:**

A.  Place the frozen banana slices in a large high-speed blender and pour in the almond milk.

B.  Stir in the vanilla extract and blitz until everything is creamy and delicious. It will take around 2 minutes.

C.  Serve right away or freeze it for later.

# 2. Coconut Banana Ice Cream

Adding a little coconut milk to your ice cream recipe is a fun and delicious way to enjoy hot summer days. Also, if you like, you can change the coconut milk to coconut cream for even more reach texture.

**Time:** 10 minutes

**Servings:** 4

**The list of ingredients:**

- 5 bananas (sliced and frozen)

- 4 tablespoons coconut milk

- 1/2 teaspoon vanilla extract

**Methods:**

A. Place the frozen banana slices in a large high-speed blender and pour in the coconut milk.

B. Stir in the vanilla extract and blitz until everything is creamy and delicious. It will take around 2 minutes.

C. Serve right away or freeze it for later.

# 3. Pineapple Ice Cream

Ice cream recipes can be a lot of fun if you mix some fruit flavors like pineapple and frozen bananas. They are perfect together; if you want to know how that might taste. Taste this simple recipe.

**Time:** 10 minutes

**Servings:** 4

**The list of ingredients:**

- 5 bananas (sliced and frozen)
- 4 tablespoons whole milk
- 1/2 cup pineapple
- 1/2 teaspoon vanilla extract

**Methods:**

A. Place the frozen banana slices in a large high-speed blender and pour the whole milk.
B. Stir in the diced pineapple and vanilla extract, then blitz until everything is creamy and delicious. It will take around 2 minutes.
C. Serve right away or freeze it for later.

# 4. Coconut and Pineapple Ice Cream

This very classic Pina Colada flavor is an absolute hit over the summer. Just mix coconut cream with a bit of pineapple, and you will end up with a bowl full of tropical flavors. Try it out and enjoy this fantastic taste.

**Time:** 10 minutes

**Servings:** 4

**The list of ingredients:**

- 5 bananas (sliced and frozen)

- 4 tablespoons coconut cream
- 1/2 cup pineapple
- 1/2 teaspoon vanilla extract

**Methods:**

A. Place the frozen banana slices in a large high-speed blender and pour in the coconut cream.

B. Stir in the diced pineapple and vanilla extract, then blitz until everything is creamy and delicious. It will take around 2 minutes.

C. Serve right away or freeze it for later.

# 5. Peanut Butter Ice Cream

If you are a foodie, you should know that bananas and peanut butter are very well together. Make this fantastic ice cream recipe and enjoy it during the summer.

**Time:** 10 minutes

**Servings:** 4

**The list of ingredients:**

- 5 bananas (sliced and frozen)
- 4 tablespoons whole milk

- 2 tablespoons maple syrup

- 1/2 cup smooth peanut butter

- 1/2 teaspoon vanilla extract

**Methods:**

A. Place the frozen banana slices in a large high-speed blender and pour the whole milk.

B. Stir in the maple syrup, peanut butter, and vanilla extract, then blitz until everything is creamy and delicious. It will take around 2 minutes.

C. Serve right away or freeze it for later.

# 6. Almond butter Ice Cream

If you are not a big fan of peanut butter but love almonds instead, then this lovely almond butter cream recipe is absolutely for you. Fast, decadent, and very simple to put together.

**Time:** 10 minutes

**Servings:** 4

**The list of ingredients:**

- 5 bananas (sliced and frozen)
- 4 tablespoons whole milk
- 1/2 cup almond butter
- 1/2 teaspoon vanilla extract

**Methods:**

A. Place the frozen banana slices in a large high-speed blender and pour the whole milk.

B. Stir in the almond butter and vanilla extract, then blitz until everything is creamy and delicious. It will take around 2 minutes.

C. Serve right away or freeze it for later.

# 7. Nutella Ice Cream

Having Nutella in all its forms can be a fun and delicious experience. Plus, I think you can imagine how delicious bananas and Nutella will be together, right? Make this simple but very yummy ice cream recipe.

**Time:** 10 minutes

**Servings:** 4

**The list of ingredients:**

- 5 bananas (sliced and frozen)
- 4 tablespoons whole milk
- 1/2 cup Nutella
- 1/2 teaspoon vanilla extract

**Methods:**

A. Place the frozen banana slices in a large high-speed blender and pour the whole milk.
B. Stir in the Nutella and vanilla extract, then blitz until everything is creamy and delicious. It will take around 2 minutes.
C. Serve right away or freeze it for later.

# 8. Raspberry Ice Cream

Frozen bananas and fresh raspberries are a match that will surprise you with how delicious they can be. You can also use frozen raspberries, but the fresh ones will give the best flavor.

**Time:** 10 minutes

**Servings:** 4

**The list of ingredients:**

- 5 bananas (sliced and frozen)
- 4 tablespoons whole milk
- 1 cup fresh raspberries
- 1 tablespoon honey
- 1/2 teaspoon vanilla extract

**Methods:**

A. Place the frozen banana slices in a large high-speed blender and pour the whole milk.

B. Stir in the fresh raspberries, honey, and vanilla extract, then blitz until everything is creamy and delicious. It will take around 2 minutes.

C. Serve right away or freeze it for later.

# 9. Raspberry and lemon Ice Cream

If you understand food well, you will know that raspberries and lemons are so good together to die for. We decided to use lemon juice and zest in this recipe because they will keep the banana bright and fresh as well as bring a ton of citrus flavor to this ice cream recipe.

**Time:** 10 minutes

**Servings:** 4

**The list of ingredients:**

- 5 bananas (sliced and frozen)
- 4 tablespoons whole milk
- 1 cup fresh raspberries
- 1 lemon zest
- 1/2 lemon juice
- 1 tablespoon agave syrup
- 1/2 teaspoon vanilla extract

**Methods:**

A. Place the frozen banana slices in a large high-speed blender and pour the whole milk.
B. Stir in the fresh raspberries, agave syrup, lemon juice, zest, and vanilla extract, then blitz until everything is creamy and delicious. It will take around 2 minutes.
C. Serve right away or freeze it for later.

# 10. Blueberry Ice Cream

Fresh or frozen blueberries, you can use them both in this recipe. Make sure to mix them well with the bananas, so you will have a creamy and delicious flavor.

**Time:** 10 minutes

**Servings:** 4

**The list of ingredients:**

- 5 bananas (sliced and frozen)
- 4 tablespoons whole milk

- 1 cup fresh blueberries

- 1 tablespoon honey

- 1/2 teaspoon vanilla extract

**Methods:**

A. Place the frozen banana slices in a large high-speed blender and pour the whole milk.

B. Stir in the fresh blueberries, honey, and vanilla extract, then blitz until everything is creamy and delicious. It will take around 2 minutes.

C. Serve right away or freeze it for later.

# 11. Mango Ice Cream

Mango is an excellent fruit that can be enjoyed during hot weather. Make a beautiful ice cream dessert full of flavor, incredible color, and only 5 ingredients.

**Time:** 10 minutes

**Servings:** 4

**The list of ingredients:**

- 5 bananas (sliced and frozen)
- 4 tablespoons whole milk

- 1 cup mango (cut into cubes)
- 1 tablespoon honey
- 1/2 teaspoon vanilla extract

**Methods:**

A. Place the frozen banana slices in a large high-speed blender and pour the whole milk.
B. Stir in the fresh mango, honey, and vanilla extract, then blitz until everything is creamy and delicious. It will take around 2 minutes.
C. Serve right away or freeze it for later.

# 12. Blueberry and Lemon Ice Cream

Just like raspberries and lemon or blueberries and lemon are perfect together. If you crave a ice and sweet dessert recipe, you should try out this incredible ice cream recipe that is ready in just a few minutes.

**Time:** 10 minutes

**Servings:** 4

**The list of ingredients:**

- 5 bananas (sliced and frozen)

- 4 tablespoons whole milk

- 1 cup fresh blueberries

- 1 lemon juice and zest

- 1 tablespoon honey

- 1/2 teaspoon vanilla extract

**Methods:**

A. Place the frozen banana slices in a large high-speed blender and pour the whole milk.

B. Stir in the fresh blueberries, lemon juice and zest, honey, and vanilla extract, then blitz until everything is creamy and delicious. It will take around 2 minutes.

C. Serve right away or freeze it for later.

# 13. Avocado Ice Cream

Avocados are very creamy and delicious, but if you try them in this frozen ice cream dessert, you will fall in love with avocados even more. Fast, simple, and very fresh.

**Time:** 10 minutes

**Servings:** 4

**The list of ingredients:**

- 5 bananas (sliced and frozen)
- 4 tablespoons whole milk

- 1 fresh avocado
- 1 tablespoon honey
- 1/2 teaspoon vanilla extract

**Methods:**

A. Place the frozen banana slices in a large high-speed blender and pour the whole milk.
B. Stir in the fresh avocado, honey, and vanilla extract, then blitz until everything is creamy and delicious. It will take around 2 minutes.
C. Serve right away or freeze it for later.

# 14. Peach Ice Cream

Peaches, when they are in season, are very cheap. Grab some peaches and few bananas, then whip up this incredible frozen dessert. I am sure that you will love it and enjoy it.

**Time:** 10 minutes

**Servings:** 4

**The list of ingredients:**

- 5 bananas (sliced and frozen)
- 4 tablespoons whole milk

- 3 fresh peaches
- 1 tablespoon maple syrup
- 1/2 teaspoon vanilla extract

**Methods:**

A. Place the frozen banana slices in a large high-speed blender and pour the whole milk.

B. Stir in the fresh peaches, maple syrup, vanilla extract, and blitz until everything is creamy and delicious. It will take around 2 minutes.

C. Serve right away or freeze it for later.

# 15. Apricot Ice Cream

This ice cream recipe is packed with delicious flavor. You will adore the color, the flavor, and the taste, plus it's so easy to put together. All you have to do is to blitz some super simple ingredients together, and the final result will be a tremendously ice cream recipe.

**Time:** 10 minutes

**Servings:** 4

**The list of ingredients:**

- 5 bananas (sliced and frozen)
- 4 tablespoons whole milk
- 6 fresh apricots
- 1 tablespoon maple syrup
- 1/2 teaspoon vanilla extract

**Methods:**

A. Place the frozen banana slices in a large high-speed blender and pour the whole milk.
B. Stir in the fresh apricots, maple syrup, and vanilla extract, then blitz until everything is creamy and delicious. It will take around 2 minutes.
C. Serve right away or freeze it for later.

# 16. Strawberry Ice Cream

Banana and strawberries are perfect for milkshakes, ice creams, and ice creams. It's creamy, refreshing, and so yummy. They are so good together that you can't have enough of this duo.

**Time:** 10 minutes

**Servings:** 4

**The list of ingredients:**

- 5 bananas (sliced and frozen)

- 4 tablespoons whole milk

- 1 cup fresh diced strawberries

- 1 tablespoon maple syrup

- 1/2 teaspoon vanilla extract

**Methods:**

A. Place the frozen banana slices in a large high-speed blender and pour the whole milk.

B. Stir in the fresh strawberries, maple syrup, and vanilla extract, then blitz until everything is creamy and delicious. It will take around 2 minutes.

C. Serve right away or freeze it for later.

# 17. Plum Ice Cream

Bananas and plums, even though they don't sound like a matching duo but they are delicious and so well together. You can substitute the maple syrup with honey or agave for a slightly different taste.

**Time:** 10 minutes

**Servings:** 4

**The list of ingredients:**

- 5 bananas (sliced and frozen)

- 4 tablespoons whole milk

- 4 stoned plums

- 1 tablespoon maple syrup

- 1/2 teaspoon vanilla extract

**Methods:**

A. Place the frozen banana slices in a large high-speed blender and pour the whole milk.

B. Stir in the fresh plums, maple syrup, and vanilla extract, then blitz until everything is creamy and delicious. It will take around 2 minutes.

C. Serve right away or freeze it for later.

# 18. Passion Fruit Ice Cream

It's amazing how the taste of passion fruit perfectly aligns with the smooth and creamy flavor of the bananas. This will probably be the best ice cream recipe you have ever made and tried.

**Time:** 10 minutes

**Servings:** 4

**The list of ingredients:**

- 5 bananas (sliced and frozen)

- 4 tablespoons whole milk
- 2 passion fruits (pulp only)
- 1 tablespoon maple syrup
- 1/2 teaspoon vanilla extract

**Methods:**

A. Place the frozen banana slices in a large high-speed blender and pour the whole milk.
B. Stir in the fresh passion fruit, maple syrup, and vanilla extract, then blitz until everything is creamy and delicious. It will take around 2 minutes.
C. Serve right away or freeze it for later.

# 19. Cherry Ice Cream

You can use frozen cherries, fresh cherries, or even cherry pie filling for this ice cream recipe. Each of these will work fine, and you will adore the taste of creamy, ice cream dessert served with a cup of coffee.

**Time:** 10 minutes

**Servings:** 4

**The list of ingredients:**

- 5 bananas (sliced and frozen)

- 4 tablespoons whole milk

- 1 cup cherries (pitted and diced into pieces)

- 1 tablespoon maple syrup

- 1/2 teaspoon vanilla extract

**Methods:**

A. Place the frozen banana slices in a large high-speed blender and pour the whole milk.

B. Stir in the fresh cherries, maple syrup, and vanilla extract, then blitz until everything is creamy and delicious. It will take around 2 minutes.

C. Serve right away or freeze it for later.

# 20. Lime Ice Cream

Having a simple ice cream recipe will bring maximum enjoyment while eating. At the same time, you will feel the creamy and sweet bananas and the sour notes from the lime zest and juice—just gorgeous.

**Time:** 10 minutes

**Servings:** 4

**The list of ingredients:**

- 5 bananas (sliced and frozen)

- 2 limes juice and zest

- 1 tablespoon maple syrup

- 1/2 teaspoon vanilla extract

**Methods:**

A. Place the frozen banana slices in a large high-speed blender and pour in the lime juice.

B. Stir in the lime zest, maple syrup, and vanilla extract, then blitz until everything is creamy and delicious. It will take around 2 minutes.

C. Serve right away or freeze it for later.

# 21. Forest Fruit Ice Cream

Just mix your mixed berries with the frozen bananas; you will end up with purple magic. Delicious, simple, and unique how fast this recipe can be done.

**Time:** 10 minutes

**Servings:** 4

**The list of ingredients:**

- 5 bananas (sliced and frozen)
- 4 tablespoons whole milk

- 1 cup forest fruits
- 1 tablespoon agave syrup
- 1/2 teaspoon vanilla extract

**Methods:**

A. Place the frozen banana slices in a large high-speed blender and pour the whole milk.

B. Stir in the fresh cherries, agave syrup, and vanilla extract, then blitz until everything is creamy and delicious. It will take around 2 minutes.

C. Serve right away or freeze it for later.

# 22. Kiwi Ice Cream

Light green color, tiny black dots, and fantastic taste are the words that will describe this following ice cream combination. Use your kiwis in a fancy way and prepare this amazing dessert.

**Time:** 10 minutes

**Servings:** 4

**The list of ingredients:**

- 5 bananas (sliced and frozen)

- 4 tablespoons whole milk
- 3 kiwis (peeled and diced into chunks)
- 1 tablespoon agave syrup
- 1/2 teaspoon vanilla extract

**Methods:**

A. Place the frozen banana slices in a large high-speed blender and pour the whole milk.
B. Stir in the fresh kiwis, agave syrup, and vanilla extract, then blitz until everything is creamy and delicious. It will take around 2 minutes.
C. Serve right away or freeze it for later.

# 23. Caramel Ice Cream

If you want to go extra with calories but want to taste something unique, this caramel ice cream recipe is for you. You can make your caramel sauce, but store-bought will work perfectly here.

**Time:** 10 minutes

**Servings:** 4

**The list of ingredients:**

- 5 bananas (sliced and frozen)

- 4 tablespoons whole milk

- 1/2 cup caramel sauce

- 1/2 teaspoon vanilla extract

**Methods:**

A. Place the frozen banana slices in a large high-speed blender and pour the whole milk.

B. Stir in the caramel sauce and vanilla extract, then blitz until everything is creamy and delicious. It will take around 2 minutes.

C. Serve right away or freeze it for later.

# 24. Oreo Ice Cream

Yes, this dessert is heaven to all of you who love Oreos. Just through some crushed Oreos in your high-speed blender and blitz just until the bananas are creamy and delicious. Add extra crushed Oreos if you want chunky ice cream.

**Time:** 10 minutes

**Servings:** 4

**The list of ingredients:**

- 5 bananas (sliced and frozen)

- 4 tablespoons whole milk

- 10 crushed Oreo cookies

- 1/2 teaspoon vanilla extract

**Methods:**

A. Place the frozen banana slices in a large high-speed blender and pour the whole milk.

B. Stir in the crushed Oreos and vanilla extract, then blitz until everything is creamy and delicious. It will take around 2 minutes. Add more crushed Oreos for crunchier consistency.

C. Serve right away or freeze it for later.

# 25. Chocolate Chip Cookie Ice Cream

This American classic can be made into a ice cream so quickly only by adding some crushed chocolate chip cookies to your ice cream base.

**Time:** 10 minutes

**Servings:** 4

**The list of ingredients:**

- 5 bananas (sliced and frozen)
- 4 tablespoons whole milk
- 5 chocolate chips
- 1/2 teaspoon vanilla extract

**Methods:**

A. Place the frozen banana slices in a large high-speed blender and pour the whole milk.

B. Stir in the vanilla extract and blitz until everything is creamy and delicious. It will take around 2 minutes. Stir in the crushed cookies and mix just until combined.

C. Serve right away or freeze it for later.

# 26. Chocolate and caramel Ice Cream

Chocolate and caramel have always been among the best matches you can find in recipes. This chocolate and caramel ice cream screams summer.

**Time:** 10 minutes

**Servings:** 4

**The list of ingredients:**

- 5 bananas (sliced and frozen)
- 4 tablespoons whole milk

- 1 tablespoon cocoa powder

- 1/4 cup caramel sauce

- 1/2 teaspoon vanilla extract

**Methods:**

A. Place the frozen banana slices in a large high-speed blender and pour the whole milk.

B. Stir in the caramel sauce, cocoa powder, and vanilla extract, then blitz until everything is creamy and delicious. It will take around 2 minutes.

C. Serve right away or freeze it for later.

# 27. Chocolate and cherry Ice Cream

If you love regular ice cream, you should know the Cherry Garcia Flavor. That flavor inspired this ice cream, but we changed the things and added cocoa powder for chocolate flavor and chocolate chips for extra crunch.

**Time:** 10 minutes

**Servings:** 4

**The list of ingredients:**

- 5 bananas (sliced and frozen)

- 4 tablespoons whole milk

- 1 tablespoon cocoa powder

- 1 cup pitted cherries

- 1/2 cup chocolate chips

- 1/2 teaspoon vanilla extract

**Methods:**

A. Place the frozen banana slices in a large high-speed blender and pour the whole milk.

B. Stir in the cocoa powder, cherries, and vanilla extract, then blitz until everything is creamy and delicious. Stir in the chocolate chips and mix just until combined. It will take around 2 minutes.

C. Serve right away or freeze it for later.

# 28. Bloody Orange Ice Cream

Bloody oranges tend to have a more intense flavor and decadent taste. If you are a high fan of the orange season, you can make this tremendous ice cream even during the summer. You can use regular oranges if you don't have access to bloody ones.

**Time:** 10 minutes

**Servings:** 4

**The list of ingredients:**

- 5 bananas (sliced and frozen)

- 4 tablespoons whole milk
- 2 peeled bloody oranges
- 1/2 teaspoon vanilla extract

**Methods:**

A. Place the frozen banana slices in a large high-speed blender and pour the whole milk.

B. Stir in the blood oranges and vanilla extract, then blitz until everything is creamy and delicious. It will take around 2 minutes.

C. Serve right away or freeze it for later.

# 29. Peanut butter and chocolate Ice Cream

Peanut butter, chocolate, and caramel make a delicious snickers flavor. If you want to make a complete snickers ice cream, drizzle some caramel sauce on top of your scoops, and you will achieve that. Peanut butter and chocolate are fine together, and you will adore them.

**Time:** 10 minutes

**Servings:** 4

**The list of ingredients:**

- 5 bananas (sliced and frozen)
- 4 tablespoons whole milk
- 1 tablespoon cocoa powder
- 2 tablespoons peanut butter
- 1/2 teaspoon vanilla extract

**Methods:**

A. Place the frozen banana slices in a large high-speed blender and pour the whole milk.

B. Stir in the cocoa powder, peanut butter, and vanilla extract, then blitz until everything is creamy and delicious. It will take around 2 minutes.

C. Serve right away or freeze it for later.

# 30. Coconut and Chocolate Ice Cream

For a bounty flavor, mix coconut and chocolate into your ice cream base, and you will be happier when you bite even the first spoon of this decadent dessert. We use cocoa powder for a chocolate flavor, but you can also use melted chocolate for an even richer taste.

**Time:** 10 minutes

**Servings:** 4

**The list of ingredients:**

- 5 bananas (sliced and frozen)

- 4 tablespoons whole milk

- 1 tablespoon cocoa powder

- 1/4 cup toasted coconut

- 1/2 teaspoon vanilla extract

**Methods:**

A. Place the frozen banana slices in a large high-speed blender and pour the whole milk.

B. Stir in the cocoa powder, coconut flakes, and vanilla extract, then blitz until everything is creamy and delicious. Stir in the chocolate chips and mix just until combined. It will take around 2 minutes.

C. Serve right away or freeze it for later.